ART CONCEPTS
FOR CHILDREN

by carol brown small

Carol Brown Small

...Reserved

ISBN 0-938267-04-3

Library of Congress Cataloging-in-Publication Data

Small, Carol Brown, 1947-
    Art concepts for children.

    Includes index.
    Summary: Explains art principles so they can be
used in art explorations. Includes discussions of
the brain, color, drawing, and media.
    1. Art--Study and teaching (Elementary)--United
States--Juvenile literature. [1. Art] I. Title.
N362.S57   1989   700   89-14917
ISBN 0-938267-04-3

Printed in the United States of America

Bold Productions
P.O. Box 152281, Arlington, TX 76015
(817) 468-9924

Dedication

To my Children

TABLE OF CONTENTS

INTRODUCTION FOR PARENTS

This book is for children. The concepts, or ideas, are not about *children's* art, however. They apply to all art. Children bring their own perspective to art, but the principles of art are universal. What works for the adult, professional artist also works for the young, part-time student of art. Thus, *Art Concepts for Children* explains principles so that children can use them in their art explorations.

This book is an overview of art study which allows the student to make choices for experimenting with selected art forms. The subjects covered are those which children can explore with little adult instruction and assistance. Although an adult partner is ideal for assembling supplies and following recipes, he/she may actually be a hindrance during the creative process. I recommend that if a parent works with the child, that he/she do so as an *art partner*, i.e., an equal.

Art Concepts for Children is written for children in the upper elementary grades. It may also be of interest to junior high students, especially if the subject of left brain/right brain theory is new to this group.

Parents who do not have a background in art can use this book as a quick self-tutor. The material can easily be adapted for oral discussion with children, enhancing a walk through an art museum. Many of the projects and recipes can be adapted for the smaller hands and shorter attention spans of younger children in the family.

> ## MESSAGE TO YOUNG ARTISTS
>
> Please ask for adult help whenever your
> work calls for the use of sprays, heat, or any
> supplies that have a strong smell.

GROWING AS AN ARTIST

Why Art?

Why do we humans care so much about art? And when do we start caring ... after we take care of our basic survival needs ... or while we are taking care of those needs? These are the first questions to ask about art, and the last to answer. In fact, we don't ever answer them fully. We just offer theories as to the why and when of art, without hope of ever having proof for final answers.

Without trying to cover all the theories (and definitely without trying to prove any of them), let's explore some areas of <u>why</u> and <u>when</u> which apply directly to you and your environment. The ideas in this chapter are just ideas, not rules and not laws. You may agree with some of them — the ones that "sound" like you — and disagree with others.

Why art? Because we can use art for self-expression. Self-expression simply means showing how we feel and think. Human beings love to act out thoughts and emotions. We express them to other humans, and sometimes just for ourselves. Of course, art is not the only means of self-expression. We also use speech, music, theatre, and physical action to express ourselves.

Rendering art — *doing* art — is one way to express feelings. But so is appreciating art. When a person admires someone else's artwork, and maybe even buys it, he may be using that art for self-expression. Is that self-expression by remote control? Yes, but it may be just as satisfying as doing the art on your own.

4

Here's an example: if you draw a fantasy land showing your ideal belongings, you have used art for self-expression. And if you buy a poster of a unicorn (or a red Lambourghini) you would like to own, you have also used art for self-expression.

When?

When do we humans take the time for art? Actually, we build art into our everyday life. When we buy clothing and shoes we make art decisions. When we buy toys we make art decisions. Even when we get haircuts we make art decisions. We don't wait until we are rich to take the time for art. And we don't wait until we have graduated from school or retired from careers to take the time for art.

Although many people are not aware of how much art — which includes decoration and design— is in their lives, it certainly is there.

As a student of art you may be tempted to separate art into 2 areas: formal art and everyday art. This is a common separation, but not a necessary one. Look for the overlapping of the 2 areas instead, and you will find yourself enjoying art doubly.

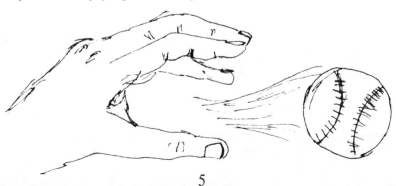

5

Growing as an Artist

These tips will help you grow as an artist. Remind yourself of them often.

● Give yourself permission to be creative.

● Think about the process, not the product. Think about what you are *doing*, not what you think the artwork should look like.

● Try as many materials as possible. Don't hold back because you have never used a medium. Go ahead and experiment even with "difficult" media such as watercolors. Remember, your goal is to *try* as many as possible, not to master them.

● Watch for happy accidents. Sometimes the media* will present you with a surprise. Watch closely and you can learn either how to do it again or how to let it happen again.

● Trust your instincts. Artists face many choices and decisions. In fact, you may find so many choices that you may feel confused and want help. But your growth as an artist depends on making those choices on your own. Don't worry about making wrong choices because even a "wrong" choice may produce a very happy accident. If making a decision is hard, follow your first instinct; it will probably be a good place to start.

* Media are the art materials. The word "medium" means just 1 material. You might say, "My favorite medium is charcoal." Or, to list more materials, you might say, "My favorite media are charcoal, pastel, and colored pencil."

Creativity

Creativity is not limited to the arts. It is easy to see in art, music, dance, theatre, and literature. But creativity is just as important in science, mathematics, engineering, politics, and so forth. In these areas, creativity may be called "innovation," or some other word, but it is still creativity.

Everyone knows the feeling of creative discovery: it is the moment that you say "Aha!" or "I've got it!" and feel wonderful at finally having the answer to a problem. Of course, an "Aha!" can happen in math class as easily as in art class.

The "Aha!" moment may be the best remembered part of the creative process, but it comes near the end of that process. Creativity begins with the questions you ask when you first face a problem or begin a project.

Sometimes the question stage drags on and on. You may feel upset at having unanswered questions, but part of you knows to let the questions rumble around in your brain for a while.

Finally, after your brain has "cooked" the problem for a while, you discover the answer. The "Aha!" comes to you very quickly.

This creative process may take a few minutes or several months. Remember the first step in the process: asking questions. If there is a single way to "increase creativity" it is to ask more questions. So, ask away!

Preserving Artwork

Spray fixative and spray plastic are available at art supply stores. They can be sprayed over drawings and paintings to preserve the artwork. A cheaper spray, but also effective, is hair spray. (Ask an adult to help.)

Small drawings and paintings can be laminated (sealed between two pieces of plastic). Most schools have laminating machines, and a lot of quick printing shops have them, too.

The traditional way to preserve artwork is to frame it behind glass. If you take your art to a frame shop for this, ask that only acid-free mat board be used.

Ideally, your drawing or painting should be done on acid-free paper. (It is the acid in paper that turns it brown and eventually makes it crumble.) This paper is more expensive and may be available only in art supply stores.

Since cardboard is highly acidic, don't mount your artwork on cardboard. If you do, the acid will eventually transfer to your artwork and damage it.

The best way to preserve your artwork is to use only the best materials. This is not always possible, since the best is also the most expensive. You can, however, take some of the steps above to extend the life of artwork made from less expensive materials.

Above all, respect your artwork. Protect it from creases, dirt, and spills.

Building a Portfolio

A portfolio is a collection of your own artwork. It may be in a real portfolio case, or in a large photograph album, or in a large manila folder, or in a box, or in a folded poster board.

Artists use portfolios to show samples of their best work. You may want to place your "best" work in your portfolio. Or you may use your portfolio for samples of a year's work, or to show samples of your work in a particular medium.

So, you may have several folders, each marked for one year. Or you may have one folder for pencil drawings, another folder for paintings, and so forth.

You almost certainly will not be able to save everything you make, especially fragile things like paper sculptures and mobiles. But you *can* photograph them and put the photos in your portfolio.

Sign and date all your artwork. You may have to do that on the back of some pieces, but remember to do it. Many artists sign their work in pencil. This is a personal choice.

You can make up titles for your art pieces, if you like. But don't worry about naming everything. As you may have noticed in art museums and galleries, a lot of artwork is labelled "Untitled."

Left Brain/Right Brain

We can all do math, we can all do creative writing, we can all play basketball, we can all paint. We can even learn to do those things well. Yes, *all* of us can learn to do them well. But as you have no doubt noticed by now in your lifetime, some people achieve at certain tasks more easily than do other people.

Spelling "comes naturally" to one student, but is very difficult for another. Long division can be done mentally by one student, but requires a notebook of scratch paper for the next student. And art? Well, some people just seem to have been born with a #8 flat brush in hand.

Is the "born artist" really more talented, more creative, more gifted than the average art student? No. Those 3 things — talent, creativity, and giftedness — are not measureable items. Since you cannot measure them, you also cannot compare one person's traits with another person's. They are *subjective* traits which can only be discussed in terms of the individual. So, you can say about yourself: "My talent is more developed than it was a year ago," or "I think more creatively when I'm relaxed. " But you cannot compare yourself to another student, because every person's traits are unique.

Then how can we explain a "born artist" in objective terms? By looking at the artist's brain. He probably has a dominant right brain. That means the right side of his brain is where he does his best "thinking." Of course, his left brain is active, too, because it handles a lot of thinking for reading and talking and so forth. But when it comes to drawing or painting or sculpting, this artist's right brain just kicks in and creates.

By comparison, the "born teacher" has a dominant left brain. He is a good speaker and can use words to explain difficult subjects to students. He is very comfortable with left brain activities, like using symbols and logic. See page 12 for more comparisons of left and right brain activity.

Is everyone set up for just left brain or just right brain work? No! Even if one type of work comes more easily, you can learn to do the other.

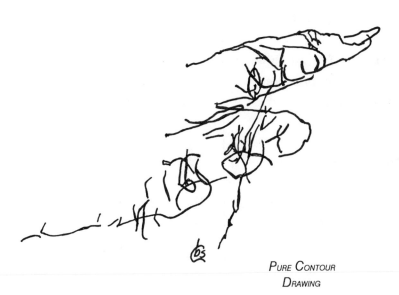

PURE CONTOUR
DRAWING

Left Brain Talk	Right Brain Talk
Giving directions:	
"Go 3 blocks east; turn right at the light; look for the big elm tree; turn at the next alley."	"Let me draw you a map."
Setting time limits:	
"I will have the report finished at a quarter of three, or 2:45."	"I will have it ready around mid-afternoon."
Judging a situation:	
"I will need to see the statistics before I know if this is safe."	"My intuition tells me that this is a safe situation."
Drawing conclusions:	
"The facts of the case make it clear that we sighted a UFO."	"I can't prove what I saw, but I believe it was a UFO."

WHEN TAPPING INTO THE RIGHT SIDE OF THE BRAIN,
THE ARTIST PRODUCES A PURE CONTOUR DRAWING OF A HAND.

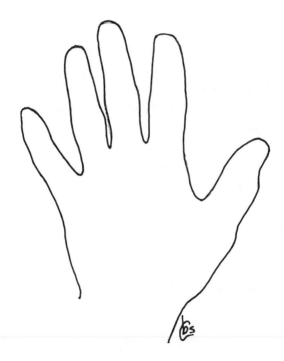

THE LEFT SIDE OF THE BRAIN IS A KNOW-IT-ALL:
"LEARN HOW TO DRAW A HAND? HOW SILLY ... I KNOW HOW TO DRAW A HAND!"
(AND PROCEEDS TO DRAW A FAMILIAR SYMBOL OF A HAND)

Learning to Use Both Sides of the Brain

Since this is a book about art, we won't consider right brain people who want to improve accounting skills. We'll just talk about left brain people who want to improve art skills.

It's really not *skills* that make art better, although left brain people tend to look for techniques that improve performance. In art, improvement comes from new awareness, or from insight, or from simply seeing in a new way.

A right brain artist may not be able to explain these concepts in words, because words don't always work in right brain activity. Some thinking in the right brain really is *unexplainable*. The only way you can learn about these concepts is to experience them, not read about them.

Use the experiment on page 16 to tap into your right brain. Don't try to make sense of the experiment. Don't even think about its purpose. Just let yourself *do* the exercise without thinking about it.

This idea of not thinking about what you are doing is really nothing new for you. When you *trust your instinct* about a new friend, you are making a judgement in your right brain. When you *lose track of time* on a bicycle ride, your right brain is allowing you to ride on and on without concern.

Although you may use your left brain mostly

when learning to play basketball, for example, you know when to turn off the left brain and turn on the right when it is time for fast play. Since your left brain is good at going through steps and figuring things out part-by-part, it can really slow you down. Once you know a game's rules, you need to be able to look at the whole situation and react to it quickly. Your right brain does that for you. The worst thing you can do is tap into the left brain for a careful analysis, at least not when the clock is running.

You can surely remember letting go and just reacting in situations like these. Art in the right brain is exactly the same.

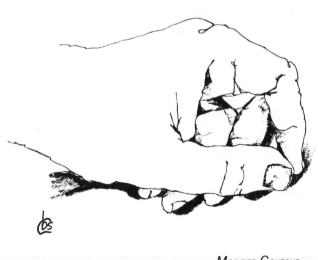

Modified Contour Drawing

Letting the Right Brain Take Over

This exercise will encourage your right brain to take over operations. Your left brain will not be able to make much sense of the exercise and won't even try to direct the drawing.

Follow the rules below in drawing the seated young man on page 17. No, there's no mistake — the young man is *supposed* to be upside-down. Without turning the book around, draw him on a separate piece of paper. Start with a box 3½" wide by 6" tall.

Rules

- Work on one line at a time.
- Don't worry about the whole drawing.
- Leave the drawing upside-down until finished.
- Draw exactly what you see.
- Don't talk about it, either out loud or silently.

Don't be put off by the complicated look of this drawing. Draw just one short line at a time, from one point to another. Remember dot-to-dot workbooks you filled in when you were younger? Use the same technique here.

Drawing this way confuses the left brain. And when confused, the left brain shuts down.

Upside-Down Drawing

Haven't I Met You Before?

If you have done the exercise on page 16, you may be feeling that right brain work is not so unfamiliar to you, after all. You have used that right brain before. In fact, you have used it every day of your life.

No one is totally left brain, or totally right brain. The two halves work together all the time, without planning. When you are faced with a task, your brain very quickly assigns it to the half that can do the job most easily.

Since you don't have to make a conscious decision about which side of your brain will be doing the work, you could go through your whole life never realizing that there are two sides with different styles. And since the two sides send messages back and forth in split seconds, there's no easy way to sort out which is which, anyway.

But the exercise on page 16 certainly made you aware of turning off the left brain and turning on the right. And the experience may have felt familiar. It is the same feeling you have when you suddenly know the answer to a problem that you haven't been able to figure out. And it is the same feeling you have when you *play by instinct* on a video game you've never seen before.

The words instinct and intuition are the best terms to describe the thinking we do in the right brain. The thinking is done without words, without going through a-b-c steps, and without worrying over facts.

Since school is a place where we do a lot of left brain activities, and we measure our intelligence according to how we do there, it is easy to assume that right brain thinking is "less" intelligent than left brain thinking. But this is certainly not true. Right brain activity is just as important as left brain, but because it is so hard to describe it doesn't lend itself to measurement.

How would you measure intuition? How would you measure creativity? These cannot be measured and compared, so they don't make it onto the report cards. But the "silent" abilities of the right brain are every bit as capable of being brilliant.

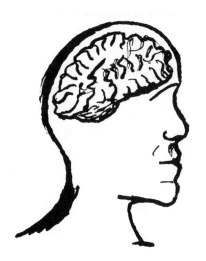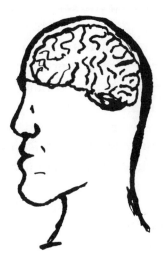

When Art is a Problem

The 10-year-old in all of us screams out terrible things like "This looks crummy!" and "Where did I go to art school — on Mars?" Being 10 (or 11 or 12) and having to look at your own art, especially in public, can be devastating. Suddenly you don't like your drawing anymore. What used to look just fine now looks unrealistic.

Sadly, most people give up art when they find realism "impossible." You probably know many adults who haven't drawn a picture since childhood. Oh, they may make a doodle here and there, but no real drawing.

If you are very lucky you may learn to draw things realistically on your own. By chance or maybe because right brain thinking comes more easily to you, your right brain directs your hand to draw exactly what your eye sees. That right brain "chance" drawing is successful, so you allow the right brain to take over the next time, too. Pretty soon, you are drawing everything realistically. With confidence building, you also feel free to try any type of drawing, not just realism.

If you have not been so lucky, and find yourself frustrated at not drawing realistically, you can change things two ways:

First, practice switching over to right brain every time you draw. Use the exercise on page 16, and make up your own, similar exercises. You will see an immediate difference in your work. Within a few weeks or months, you will see great improvement in your realistic drawings. You can go further with "drawing on the right side of the brain," by reading books by Betty Edwards and by working with art teachers who agree with right brain theory.

Second, take off the "realism" pressure. Although realism may be your goal in art, take a break from it by going in the other direction: abstract. Since an abstract painting (or any other abstract art form) is neither realistic nor unrealistic, you can't criticize your work as easily. You will find yourself enjoying color and design for their own sake, not as measures of how good an artist you are.

If you begin a study of abstract art you will learn that abstract is just as serious an art form as any other. At first glance, it looks easy ... a blob here and a blob there and you have an abstract painting, right? It's not that simple. Good abstract art is just as meaningful and emotional as a detailed sculpture, so a good abstract may take about as long to complete. But in one sense abstract is easier: it is often spontaneous. That is, you may find yourself suddenly trying a new color or design on the spur of the moment. Abstract gives you the freedom to do this.

Objective abstract is representational: it is related to a real thing, even though the object is drawn or painted unrealistically. Non-objective abstract is non-representational: it is not tied to a real object. Jackson Pollock's paintings are famous non-objective abstracts. In his "action paintings" he dribbled and poured paint onto the canvas. You might want to try action painting!

21

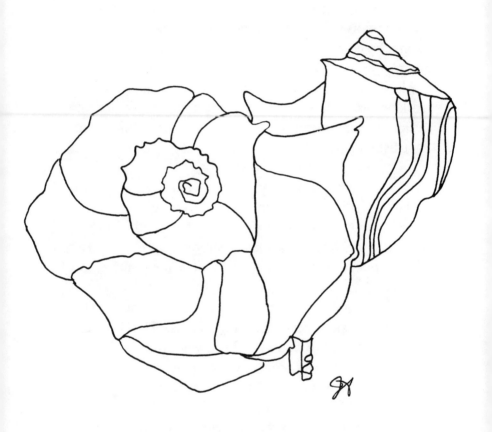

*Objective Abstract
Drawing*

Non-objective Abstract

Brain in Training

To draw realistically, you must have a model in front of you or have the image etched in your memory.

To create such a memory, you must observe and draw your subject as often as you can. You could call this "etching" on your brain.

ordinary brown paper bags are fun to draw

Keep a sketchbook not only for drawing,
but also for making notes of your thoughts.

ELEMENTS AND PRINCIPLES OF ART

Art Elements

Just as chemistry claims a set of elements, so does art. In formal art study we list these elements:

● line — Straight and curved, lines may be the edges that we immediately notice, or even "invisible" edges going between or behind objects. One of the most important line concepts is direction. If a line is horizontal it suggests quiet (maybe because when our bodies are horizontal *we* are quiet, or asleep). A vertical line, standing up, suggests awake, alert, ready for something to happen. A diagonal line suggests that something already is happening.

● shape — An object's outside form is its shape. The basis of all shape/form is a small number of geometric shapes.

● texture — An object's look and feel is the texture. Of course, you are not allowed to feel some art objects, in museums for example, and so you must rely on what you can see of the texture. Texture can be described with adjectives like these: smooth, rough, grainy, soft, hard, fuzzy, etc.

● color — The colors we see are really reflections of light. So when we create paint with a pigment, we are making a liquid that absorbs or reflects certain lengths of light rays. (In a totally dark room, nothing has color because there is no light.)

● space — Forms fit together to make a drawing's spaces. See page 45 for more information.

26

• value — The lightness or darkness of an element is called its value. Your eye can probably see more than 40 low and high values of a color. Low values are the dark shades of a color created when black is added. High values are the light tints of a color created when white is added.

COPYRIGHT

Copyright isn't often mentioned in formal art study, but every artist should protect his or her creations with this simple symbol: ©.

The symbol means "copyrighted" and protects your work from use without your permission.

On the back of this book's title page, my copyright notice appears as:

Copyright © 1989 by Carol Brown Small

although just "Copyright" or just "©" is adequate as long as the year and the name are included.

Art Principles

As you continue to study art you will come across many different lists of art principles. The list on this page is the one I use, but it is no more right nor wrong than any other list.

- unity/harmony — When we see an artwork's whole pattern before noticing its individual elements, then the artist has achieved "unity."

- rhythm/repetition — Rhythm refers to how the eye moves across an artwork. Repeating shapes and patterns (regular, alternating, or progressive) helps build rhythm.

- movement — Movement in an artwork is an illusion created by the artist. Kinetic sculpture is the exception: the movement is real, not an illusion.

- emphasis — An artwork's focal point provides emphasis. It may be *the* most important element in the work, or several focal points working together to keep the viewer interested. A focal point is simply an element or area on which the eye *focuses*.

- balance — We humans like balance in our bicycle riding, our diets, *and* our artwork. Symmetry is a common way to achieve balance, but not the only way. One other way is asymmetrical balance.

- proportion — Proportion refers to how a part of a drawing fits into the whole of the drawing.

Print from Etching

*The principles of art
are applied to all media,
not just drawing.*

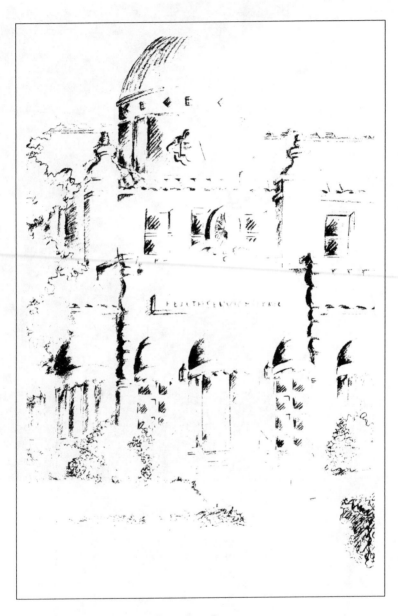

PERSPECTIVE DRAWING

Perspective

Perspective is all illusion — the illusion of three dimensions drawn on a two-dimensional surface. Your drawing paper is two dimensions: up-down, and across. The third dimension, depth, is missing.

Artists have developed several different methods of drawing perspective over the last several hundred years. Some methods are very complicated.

In modern times, some artists have fiddled with perspective on purpose, to distort shapes. And some artists have completely ignored all rules of perspective.

Perspective is difficult to learn on your own. You may have your first introduction to it in junior high art classes. A book like <u>Perspective</u> by J. M. Parramon is also helpful.

MODIFIED CONTOUR DRAWING
WITH SHADING

LOOK FOR SHAPES WHEN YOU DRAW.

32

COLOR

Four Basic Properties of Color

The letters that form this little man will help you remember the four basic properties of color.

h = hue = actual color

v = value = light or dark

i = intensity = bright or dull

t = temperature = warm or cool

SHOUT IT OUT

Complementary colors are the colors opposite each other on a color wheel.

Using complements is very powerful. For example, when you use green and red next to each other in a painting, green is no longer just green; it becomes *GREEN!*

Color — History and Theories

Before the year 1200 artists had a very few colors to work with. The basics were blacks, whites, yellows, and browns, all coming from bones and wood and the earth. Fancy colors were bronze, red, blue, green and yellow; these were pastes made from the powder of ground up minerals.

Then, in the 1200's, artists and craftsmen developed many more colors by combining mineral powders. The same thing happened in the 1800's, when colorists drew upon cadmium, sulphur, charcoal, coal-tar, and more. In those days, artists often mixed their own colors, developing very personalized palettes, or sets of colors. Today, most artists rely on paint companies for ready-made paints.

Some artists invent or adopt theories about color, and others never even think about it. As a student of art, you may find yourself carefully planning colors in one painting but just making random choices for another painting.

In the 1800's artists like Monet and Seurat worked out rules for making colors harmonious in a painting. They felt that color harmony could be treated like musical harmony. They said, "Just learn the rules and all your paintings will look harmonious."

In the 1900's artists starting rejecting the theories. Today, artists feel free to use color any way they want. Since color is so tied to our emotions (even when we are not aware of that), there is no right or wrong way.

Colors as Symbols

Color is used symbolically in our speech as well as in our visual world. Here are just a few "color connotations." You can add to the list.

Red
danger (road signs)
speed (sports cars)
anger ("He saw red")
happiness & good luck (Chinese)
blood
excitement
Communist

Yellow
cowardly ("a yellow streak")
warning (road signs)
slanderous ("yellow journalism")
irritation (to some people)
cheerful, light, sunny

Green
freshness, neutrality
envious ("green with envy")
sick, seasick ("He looks green")
amateur ("He was pretty green when he started")
lucky (Irish)
money ("greenbacks")
growth, spring time

Black
very strong ("black belt")
night, might be scary
beautiful (African American)
gruesome but funny ("black comedy," "black humor")

Blue
peaceful, tranquil
cool
moody, sad ("the blues," "Blue Monday")

Primary, Secondary, and Intermediate Colors

The primary colors in painting are red, yellow, and blue. They can be mixed to make other colors, but no other colors (pigments) can be mixed to produce the primary colors.

The secondary colors are those we make when we mix the primary colors in unequal proportions. Orange, green, and violet are the secondary colors.

Red + blue = violet.
Blue + yellow = green.
Yellow + red = orange.

Intermediate colors are produced when secondary colors are mixed with primary colors. These colors are always hyphenated (spelled with a dash) and their first words are always the names of primary colors.

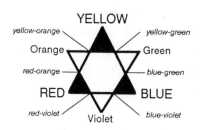

ART MATH

1 color + 1 color = many colors

Warm and Cool Colors

Different people react differently to colors, but most people have similar reactions to two groups of colors: warm and cool. Artists and designers often take advantage of this.

Warm colors: reds, oranges, and yellows.

Cool colors: blues and greens.

A designer might choose warm colors for a display of cars at a mall. Red and yellow cars would draw attention and get people excited about the cars.

But the designer might use only cool colors in decorating a dentist's waiting room. The purpose would be to calm down worried patients.

In a painting, you might plan a beach-scape in warm colors, then tone it down with a gentle blue for the water's edge. Or in a quiet, green forest scene, you might surprise your viewer with a bright yellow bird flying through the trees. Contrasts of warm and cool colors make a painting exciting.

You can also create excitement by switching the warm and cool colors. Can you make a beach with cool colors? Can you make a forest with warm colors? Your "reverse" paintings will bring out different moods, in you and in your audience.

Two-Dimensional Media: Drawing

Preparing to Draw

Drawing is an art form in itself. And it is also used in preparation for other art forms. For example, before beginning a painting an artist may make a thumbnail sketch in pencil. This is a small drawing which serves as a plan for the larger painting. If you make thumbnail sketches first, you will probably feel more confident when you begin your work.

Drawing as an art form demands much practice. You can improve your drawing ability by letting the right side of your brain direct your hand. Turn back to page 16 and review the exercise there. It will help you in letting the right brain "lead" you. Try to switch over to right brain every time you draw.

Drawing media are discussed on pages 46 - 51.

Papers are designed for each type of drawing medium, but that doesn't mean you must use only those. You can experiment with different types of paper and have many "happy accidents" while drawing. If you do want a special paper (to prevent pen and ink from spreading out or bleeding, for example) you can ask to see samples at an art supply store.

> GET READY TO DRAW
>
> Turn on some music. Spend a few minutes drawing with your "wrong" hand, then switch to your usual drawing hand. Relax.

Contour Drawing

When you look for edges of a subject, and then draw lines on paper to represent the edges, you are doing contour drawing.

The contour line is actually where two edges meet: the outside edge of the subject, and the outside edge of the background. Called *shared edges*, the result is a single contour line which can be drawn.

Drawing contour lines helps in learning to see. *Learning to see* may not make much sense to you. "Seeing comes naturally ... it's drawing I need help with!" Ah, but your drawing will come natually, once you learn to see.

Learning to see = focusing on the object as it appears, not as you think it should appear. Ribbons provide a good example.

First, make a ribbon simply by cutting a strip of paper. A strip that is 1" wide and 10" long is fine, but you can make yours fatter or longer or skinnier or shorter. Curl the ribbon by holding both ends and dragging it over the edge of a table. Then twist the ribbon several times and tape the ends to a piece of plain, flat paper.

This lovely ribbon sculpture presents many edges for you to draw. Select a view of the ribbon and start seeing and drawing. Don't worry about how the picture looks. Just draw the edges that you see.

Pure Contour Drawing

As a technique, pure contour drawing means drawing the edges of an object *without looking at the paper while you work.* Pure contour drawing is a wonderful way to focus on the *doing* of art instead of the *thinking* about art. It also removes the pressure of performing — you don't have to worry about "how it looks so far."

To begin, place your drawing hand, paper, and pencil on a table. Turn your body away so that you cannot easily look at the paper. Position the pencil point in the center of the paper (that's your last look for a long time), then turn away. Study your other hand (or another object, if you like) as the subject for drawing. Very slowly, begin drawing the contour (outside edge) of your hand. Don't think about your whole hand; don't even think about an entire finger. Simply draw each little curve and bump along the edge of your hand.

WARNING: You will feel a desire to peek.
DON'T!

When you finally look at your completed drawing, expect to see some wobbly lines ("And what part of my hand is *that* supposed to be?!?"). But also expect to see some wonderful detail work, places where you can really see the edge of your hand. Praise yourself highly for seeing and drawing those places. And praise yourself for not looking!

A PINE CONE WAS THE SUBJECT FOR THIS PURE CONTOUR DRAWING.

Modified Contour Drawing

   Draw another object, this time without turning your body away from your paper. Don't look at your work constantly. Look down for quick glances as you work, but keep your eyes trained on the subject as much as possible.

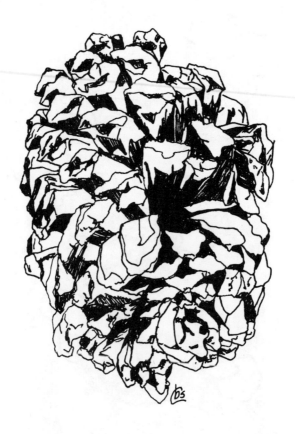

*MODIFIED CONTOUR
DRAWING OF A PINE CONE*

Positive Space and Negative Space

A drawing's positive space (sometimes the shape of an object) and negative space (sometimes the background) are equally important. This is a key concept. Once you are aware of it, drawing becomes much easier.

Draw a ladder-back chair. As you draw, notice the positive shapes of legs, rungs, and slats; the spaces between those shapes are the *negative spaces*.

The lantern drawing below is an advanced art student's work showing a combination of positive and negative spaces.

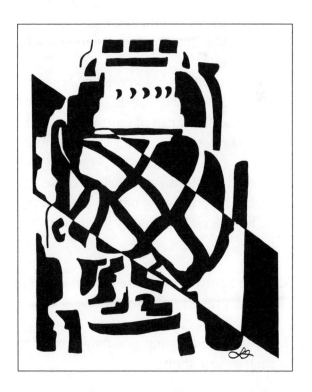

Pencil

Graphite pencil is the type you use in school. The #2 grade that teachers usually require is the next to softest grade. The scale goes from 1 to 4.

Most art pencils use another numbering system. It begins with 8B for very soft, then goes up through 7B, 6B, 5B, 4B, 3B, 2B, B, F, HB, H, 2H, 3H, 4H, 5H, 6H, 7H, to 8H. 8H is for very hard.

Soft leads work well on smooth paper. Hard leads need paper with more texture. Good watercolor paper is textured enough.

Charcoal pencil is built like a graphite pencil, but has charcoal as its point. It makes a very black line.

Colored pencil has colored lead. Sometimes called map pencils for schoolwork, these may be long or short. They come in a range of hardnesses; if you can test the pencils first, select a softer lead for easier work.

Some artists like short pencils because they feel they can control their drawing better, but others just like the feel of a long pencil. You may want to try both before you buy.

Kneaded putty erasers are the easiest to use with pencil. Art gum erasers are also good.

To preserve a drawing, you may need to spray on a fixative such as hair spray.

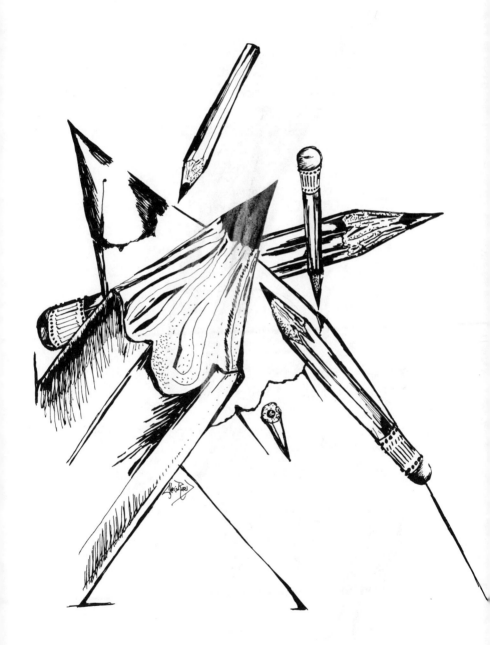

47

Pen and Ink Drawing

Pen and Ink

Old-fashioned pen and ink meant dipping a nib (point) into ink, then drawing a few lines, then dipping, then drawing. You can still do that, although most art students choose a cartridge or reservoir pen. (Many art and calligraphy classes prefer to start with dip pens, however.)

Art supply stores sell a wide variety of pens and inks. You can buy a pen that has interchangeable nibs, or several pens with different points so you don't have to change them. Pens which use ink cartridges are the cleanest to use.

Inks are known as waterproof and non-waterproof. They come in black and a range of colors.

Today, we also include felt tip and acrylic tip pens in supplies for pen and ink drawing. These pens come with different sizes and shapes of tips; some are called calligraphy pens because their tips are shaped like the nibs used with dip pens.

The inks in these pens are fast-drying. Many artists like to use the pens with water-based colors for soft effects.

Sets of markers are usually cheaper than individual ones. And many discount stores sell sets at much less than the art supply store.

Pastels, Chalks, and Charcoal

Pastels are sticks of pigment powders held together with gum arabic, a binder. They are beautiful. . . and fragile. Pictures are soft and velvety. . .and not very durable. Saving a work in pastel is a challenge. If you use high quality sticks, plus high quality paper, that will help. If you want to frame the work, mount it behind glass, but with spacers holding the plate of glass away from the pastel. If you want to save several pieces without framing them, stack them with sheets of tissue paper between them. You can weight the stack with a board on top, and the pastel will "fix" on the paper.

A spray fixative can be used on a pastel, but sometimes the colors change after being sprayed. If you do use one, start the spray off to the side, then move it onto the pastel, then off again before releasing. To determine distance and number of seconds to spray, test the fixative on a small "scratch pad" of pastel on paper. You may want to try spraying the pastel from the backside of the paper; the fixative slowly goes through the back, without making the colors dull.

Oil pastels are stronger and more durable than pure pastels. They are made with oil instead of gum arabic. This book's cover was created in this medium.

Chalks, or chalk crayons, are much harder than pastels. They are made of pigments mixed with wax or oil.

Charcoal is the oldest drawing tool in the world. Cavemen used charcoal, the sort recovered from a piece of charred wood from a fire. Today, our finest charcoal is produced from vine twigs.

Ordinary stick charcoal comes in different sizes and hardnesses. Very soft charcoal can be dusted off the paper, without even an eraser. It also smudges at the drop of a hat. Since artists usually spray a fixative on charcoal drawings, it is wise to "spray as you go," instead of waiting until the end.

Compressed charcoal is made with a binder; it is stronger, but also harder to dust off mistakes. Charcoal pencils are the least messy version to use. Kneaded putty erasers lift off mistakes, so you don't have to rub.

LOOSEN UP

Tape pastel or charcoal stick to an 18" twig. Hold onto the other end and *try* to draw. Continue for 5 minutes. This is a loosening-up exercise that will prepare you for a drawing session.

FRAMING

Framing can be expensive, but it really shows off your artwork, especially your paintings.

Light colored or natural wood frames are preferred since they do not detract from the artwork.

Lattice strips from a lumber yard are very inexpensive and make a quick frame for a painting on stretched canvas.

Turn back to page 8 for more tips on preserving artwork.

Two-Dimensional
Media:
Painting

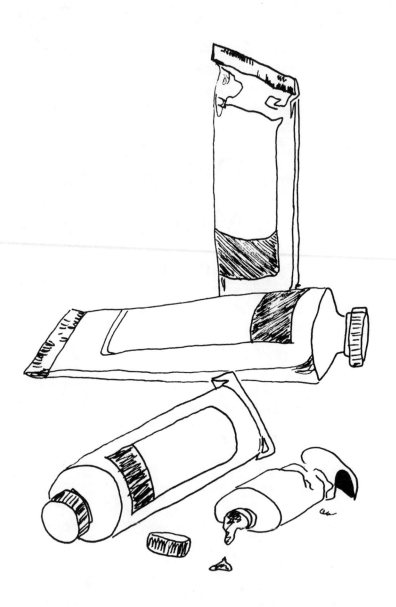

Paints

Oil paints are usually based on linseed oil, although many different oils can be used. The second most popular is poppy oil. Although oils were used in paints for many centuries, the "modern" recipe is less than 500 years old.

In art stores, ready-made oil paints are sold as Artist grade or Student grade. Grade refers to quality; you can guess which paint is more durable *and* more expensive. If purchased paint looks extra oily, it probably is. Extra oil is sometimes added to increase shelf life, that is, to make the paint last longer in the store before it is sold. To get rid of the excess oil, artists squeeze the paint out onto absorbent paper. <u>Because of their fumes, oil paints are not recommended for children.</u>

Acrylic paints are pigment in synthetic (manmade) resin. Acrylics were developed around the time of World War II. They were the first new paints to come along in more than 400 years.

With acrylics, artists can paint anywhere — even on the outside of a building — and not worry about the weather. Also, they can count on the paint's color being stable; once it dries, it is permanent. And drying is very fast, just a matter of a few minutes.

In fact, the biggest problem with acrylics is getting your brushes cleaned fast enough. You must wash brushes in water immediately after painting.

Once an acrylic painting is dry, it can actually be

washed with soap and water! The acrylic paint is water-proof, without even adding a varnish. (An outdoor mural in acrylics may be covered with an acrylic varnish, just to be on the safe side.)

Tempera paints are the oldest paints that are still in use today. Ancient artists and modern artists use the same recipe: mix equal parts of pigment and egg yolk, then add distilled water to painting consistency.

Ready-mixed tempera paints can be bought. They dry more slowly than hand-mixed paints, and come in a smaller number of colors.

Watercolors are transparent paints which are put on paper in layers, each drying before the next is added so that colors don't look "dirty." You must start with your lightest color and work to the darkest color since there is no way to "lighten" a dark color once it is on paper.

The paper is an important part of the painting, not just a hidden background. The types of paper are called hot-pressed, cold-pressed, and rough. Hot-pressed is very smooth and is difficult to work on; rough paper is so rough that it also can be difficult. Most students like to work with cold-pressed paper. A popular weight is 90 lb. (this means that a ream of the papers, or 480 sheets, weighs 90 pounds).

When you price watercolors, you can count on the best ones being the most expensive. But many companies sell watercolors in the middle range, and they are fine for learning with. You will find some as sets in boxes, some in tubes (these are semi-liquid), and some in bottles (these are liquid; you need an eyedropper to move the paint onto a palette). A bit of good news in buying watercolors: you don't need very many. The experts recommend starting with no more than 5 colors, since you can layer and mix those to make new colors. Even professional watercolorists use no more than a dozen colors.

An important technique in watercolor is the *wash*. This is watered-down watercolor. A series of washes will give you transparent layers; allow drying time between the layers.

Gouache is, in simple terms, opaque watercolor. Opaque means non-transparent, so gouache colors look "solid" when compared to watercolors. The only difference between the paints is that gouache has an added pigment: white. And white can be added to lighten colors, as you work.

Gouache can be used very thinly, so that it washes like watercolor, or in thick paste, similar to oil paint. Many watercolor techniques are used, and water-color papers work very well with gouache.

Dried gouache paintings have a flat look, not shiny. They do not reflect light as oil paintings do.

How do you say this word? Depending on what part of the country you live in, it is pronounced "gwash" (rhymes with slash) or "gwosh" (rhymes with slosh).

Brushes

Paint brushes are rated according to their size. Although the scale begins with 000 (very fine), 00, and 0, most artists would agree that 1 is as fine as most painters need. The scale goes up to 24, the largest size. Student artists often choose three sizes: 4, 8, and 12, to experiment with.

Brushes are also made and described in inches. Common sizes range from ¼" to 3" but larger sizes are available, too.

Brush shapes are bright, flat, round and filbert. A bright has short bristles with a square end. A flat looks like a bright, but with longer bristles; it can make broad strokes, or fine lines when turned on its side. A round is round-ended and good with thin paint. A filbert is like a round, but wider; it makes a smooth, rounded stroke. Another shape, fan, spreads out just like a fan; it is used to blend colors.

The best type of brush for all work is sable. The bristles are from the tail of Siberian mink. They do the best detail work; they are also very expensive.

Oil painters also like bleached hogs' hair as bristles because it holds paint well. The disadvantage of hogs' hair is that it is stiff and does not make a point very well.

Watercolor painters use sable, ox, and squirrel hair brushes. Squirrel hair is also called camel hair.

When artists use tempera paints, they use a lot of the same brushes as with watercolor, but may also use very wide brushes for covering large areas.

Synthetic bristles can make a good, inexpensive brush. Look for brushes whose bristles are shaped like the ones on expensive brushes. Shape isn't everything but it does help. Many artists use synthetics and find them as good as natural hairs.

To clean a brush, wash in cool water and soap. Rinse and squeeze out the water. Re-shape the bristles with your fingers. Store the brush lying flat. Never, never leave a brush standing in water; such treatment will ruin a brush.

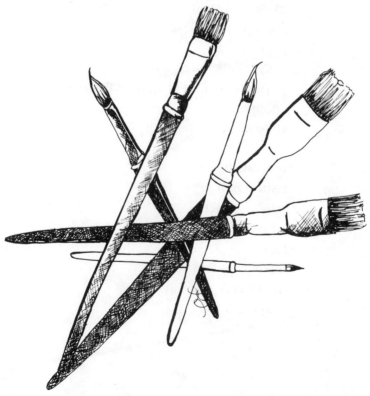

Unconventional Painting Tools

Brushes are the best known tool of painters, but certainly not the only ones. In fact, some artists would not consider the list on this page "unconventional" at all; they would tell you that they *always* use spoons, or *usually* do some fingerpainting, or *commonly* speckle paint with a toothbrush.

spoon
finger, fingertip, fingernail
toothbrush
cotton swab
eye shadow applicator
mascara brush
toothpick
stick
brayer (ink spreader)
popsicle stick or tongue depressor
sponge
shoe polish applicator
comb
hairbrush
cotton ball
pen or pencil
straw
fork
mixing spatula
paper clip
crumpled foil

Painting Surfaces

Canvas: You can buy pre-stretched canvas, or stretch your own over a wood frame. The easiest alternative is to paint on the flat, un-stretched canvas. It can even be hung on a wall like this.

Paper: Choose a heavy paper for painting. To make sure that your artwork will last many years, buy acid-free paper. This sort of paper will not turn brown and crumbly. Experiment with different types of paper: smooth, rough, shiny, matte. You will find many different types in art supply stores.

Other surfaces: Experiment with plaster, wood, plastic, metal, and fabric. A fun fabric project is to paint with acrylic paints on a T-shirt. Put a piece of cardboard inside the shirt to separate layers while you paint. Let the paint sit on the fabric for just a few minutes, then wash the shirt in plain water in the sink. When the shirt dries it will have a soft, muted, watercolor look.

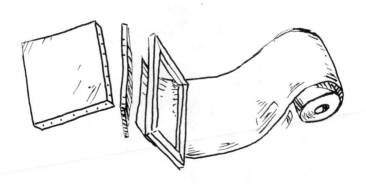

Drip Painting

Mix: 1 cup of salt
½ cup of flour
¾ cup of water

Divide into small cups or containers.

Add powdered tempera to each container,
for different colors.

If you don't have tempera to color the mixture,
use it as white paint on colored paper.

To "paint": let the mixture drip
from a brush onto paper.

Glue Paint

Add powdered tempera to white glue.
Spread the paint with sticks or toothpicks,
or squeeze it from the glue bottle
right onto the paper.

Vegetable Watercolor

Make watercolors by boiling onions in water.
Brown onion skins yield yellow or amber water.
Red onion skins yield purple or rose water.

Dry Paints

Salt Paint

Quickly stir in
¼ teaspoon of
food coloring
to about
½ cup of
salt.

Add 1 or 2
extra drops
of coloring
for darker
shades.

Spread
the salt
on a pan
to dry.
(Line the
pan with
foil or
plastic
wrap
for easy
clean up.)

Variations

Different
salts yield
different
textures:

table salt,

pickling
salt,

ice cream
salt,
etc.

Mix a salt
with dry
tempera
powder,
or with
liquid
tempera,
or both.

Sand Paint

Add about 1 tablespoon powder paint
(like tempera powder)
to ½ cup of clean sand.

Other Bases for Dry Paints

Sawdust, rice.
Color with tempera or food coloring.

Tips for Using Dry Paints

To "paint": draw a design on paper with glue,
then sprinkle salt or sand paints onto the glue.
Allow to dry, then shake off the excess salt or sand.

Spread glue from a bottle tip,
or with a brush, or with a fingertip.
Fine detail lines can be made with
a toothpick dipped in glue.

Glue may be used full-strength or watered-down.
Many artists prefer thinned glue.
The glue can also be colored:
just add powdered paint.

Dry paints can be sprinkled from shaker bottles.

Crushed Eggshells

Finely crushed eggshell can be used for texture if added to paint. Not-so-finely crushed shell can be used with glue in a collage.

Wash broken eggshell (*not* crushed yet, just the 2 or 3 large pieces you get from emptying the egg from the shell) in soap and water.

Soak the eggshell overnight in a pan of water and vinegar. This removes any egg membrane from the shell.

Dry the eggshells, then put them inside small plastic sandwich bags.

Crush the eggshells by rolling a rolling pin or a drinking glass over the bags. To experiment, crush some eggshells more than others.

To each bag, add a different food coloring or a little paint. Watch the eggshell take the color and remove when dark enough.

To dry, spread thinly on a sheet of aluminum foil.

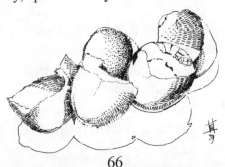

Durable Media

Use these techniques to make your artwork more durable, i.e., last longer.

If you are painting on wood, you can make tempera paint "stick" better by adding a few drops of liquid detergent.

Chalk drawings are lovely, but smeary. To prevent the otherwise inevitable, spray with hair spray, fixative, or spray plastic.* Place drawing on top of newspapers before spraying. Hold can about 12" away from the artwork and begin spraying off the side. Move spray onto the artwork and across it slowly.

More chalk tips: dip the stick of chalk into sugar water before drawing. The resulting work will last longer. Another way to make a drawing more durable is to brush the paper with buttermilk before starting. Use 2 tablespoons of buttermilk on a large piece of construction paper or cardboard.

Acrylic spray* can be used to cover work in watercolors, pastels, and pencil. Art supply stores sell two finishes: matte (flat looking) and gloss (shiny looking).

---

* All such sprays should be used by adults, and only outside or in well-ventilated areas.

Fingerpaints

Fingerpainting is like no other painting. You control the medium — the paint — *directly* and get tactile as well as visual feedback from it. Fingerpainting is also very relaxing. You can "get lost" in it. Use the suggestions below to do 3 types of fingerpainting: for the experience with no plan to preserve the work, to make a textured painting, to make a flat print from the work.

1. Just to experiment: fingerpaint on a cookie sheet or on aluminum foil or on coated (shiny) paper.

2. For a textured painting to save: fingerpaint on a heavy sheet of paper or on cardboard. Use paint thick enough so that it will not soak through the backing, but not so thick that it will cake and crack.

3. For a print: after fingerpainting a design on the table-top, press a paper on it from above. Lift the paper carefully; the result is a print (in reverse) of your design.

4. A satisfying fingerpaint may be made from liquid starch and dry paint. Make the mixing part of the finger work. Add a small amount of soap flakes for easy clean-up, especially if you are using the mixture strictly for the experience.

5. Use more than just fingers ... knuckles, palms, and fingernails can all be used to good effect.

6. If you scrupulously clean your hands and your table-top, you can enjoy pudding-paint.

7. Add texture to a liquid starch fingerpaint with one of these: sawdust, coffee grounds, rice.

When you fingerpaint you double your sensitivity to your artwork. You can feel what you see. This is quite similar to the feeling sculptors and fiber artists enjoy.

Mix and Match Fingerpaints

Possible media [choose one]	Add color [choose one]	Add texture [choose one]
liquid starch	tempera	rice
buttermilk	food coloring	coffee
whipped soapsuds (flakes + water)		salt

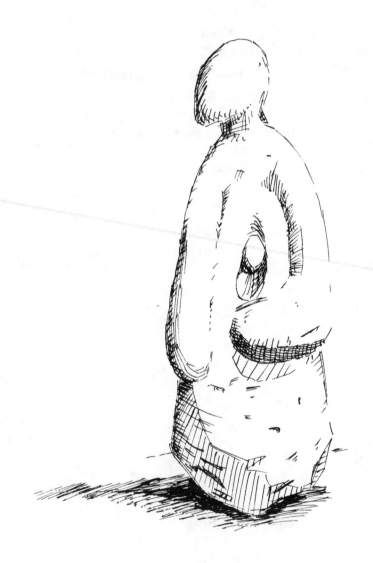

THREE-DIMENSIONAL
MEDIA

Collage — Example of Mixed Media

Collage is a well-known technique that is popular with professional artists, folk artists*, art students, and preschoolers. Collage can be just about anything you want it to be. It can have a message, or none at all. It can use related media, or random choices. It can utilize expensive items, or scraps pulled out of a trash can. Collage can be just about anything.

As an art form, collage is a type of mixed media. Mixed media simply means that you don't have to limit yourself to one medium (just watercolors, for example). Instead, you can mix up media on one canvas. You could start a landscape in acrylic paints and finish it with glued on leaves and grass. Or you could attach metal objects to a canvas and use pen and ink to write descriptions of them.

Mixed media is pretty new in the art world. Artists have been experimenting with this for fewer than a hundred years. But perhaps it really started with collage as decoration back in the 1600's. Back then, people liked to decorate their belongings with small inexpensive items that could be glued easily. Diaries and memory books often contained collages, collections of items to remember favorite days by.

Collage has been a favorite of some of our most famous artists. When Henri Matisse grew old, he had arthritis in his hands. He could not hold a paint brush

---

* A folk artist produces art and craft items with the materials in his own environment — materials that are close at hand. He works without concern for "proper" art schooling.

anymore, so he took up collage: he started making cut-paper murals. Pablo Picasso was a painter, but he sometimes put paper and cloth on his paintings.

Picasso and Georges Braque are famous for making collage an accepted art form.

You can put just about anything on a collage (see the list on page 74). Use paste or glue to attach the items to cardboard or stiff paper.

Protect the surface of a collage with spray plastic. Or, for a different look, cover the surface (if it's relatively flat) with a piece of clear contact paper. A small collage can be covered with clear plastic wrap (tape down tightly on the back).

Collage Ingredients

From the great outdoors:

leaf	stick	pebble
sand	flower petal	grass
tree bark	acorn	seed
pine needle	feather	

From the sewing box:

thread	felt scrap	yarn
ribbon	button	snap/hook
rickrack	lace	braid
fabric scrap		

From the office:

paper	reinforcement	paper clip
pencil	postage stamp	rubber band
tack	phone book page	note paper
staple	magazine page	

From the memory book:

calendar	ticket stub	postcard
letter	report card	photograph
Valentine		

From the fast food restaurant:

| straw | straw wrapper | plastic-ware |
| napkin | salt pack | pepper pack |

From the tool shed:

nail	tack	sandpaper
gasket	screw	washer
nut	bolt	sawdust
wood chip		

From the kitchen:

eggshell[1]	toothpick[2]	seed/rice
bean	macaroni	foil
twist ties	food packaging	

[1] To color: See the directions on page 66.

[2] To color: Dip into food coloring or tempera paints; dry on a sheet of aluminum foil.

Sculpture

A lot of old sculptures feature the human body. But in the last hundred years, artists have branched out and used just about every subject they could think of. This has been a big change in the history of art.

Very few old sculptures show movement. The great artist Rodin put movement into his work by showing the human body in action. But in the last hundred years, modern artists have put *real* movement in sculpture. Their new kind of work is called kinetic sculpture.

Our most famous kinetic sculptor was Alexander Calder. He experimented with many different forms of movement, but is best remembered for his mobiles which move with air currents. Mobiles are sculptures which are suspended, or hung, from above. If the movable sculpture is not suspended, but sits on a base, it is called a stabile.

Traditional sculpting media are stone, bronze, wood. Modern materials include plastic and steel. As a student you may be interested in using common, inexpensive materials such as:

pebbles, stones	cardboard	wood chips
plastic containers	wire	balsa wood
rope, string, thread	toothpicks	pipe cleaners
buttons, jewelry	fabric	paper, boxes
popsicle sticks	foam	plastic wrap

Metal sculpture may be too difficult at this stage, but you can do miniature work with soft, bendable wire. Craft stores sell very thin wire on large spools. $5 worth will make a lot of small sculpture. You can choose from different colors and sizes.

Aluminum foil also makes interesting small sculpture. You can squeeze the foil into shapes, then add details with craft items you have in the house. Thin wire may be used for the detail; that will definitely give the piece the metal look. Aluminum foil can also be painted.

Modelling

Modelling is an art form at 2 levels: some artists model objects as finished pieces of art; some artists model objects as guides for making larger scuptures. Here, we will talk about objects as finished pieces.

Media include clay (the most common one used around the world), wax, plaster, concrete, and papier-mâché. Although wax may seem unusual, ancient Greeks used it for dolls and figurines; it is really quite durable. Very often, modelling is used to produce small figures of human and animal forms. But artists should — and do — feel free to model any shape they like.

To work with clay, you must first *knead* the media. Push it, fold it over itself, roll it, just as you knead bread dough. When no air bubbles are seen, the clay is ready to work. You can put it on a potter's wheel and *throw*, or shape, a bowl. Or you can work it into a shape with your hands. By starting with a ball of clay you can form a bowl by pressing down and out with your thumbs. As a bowl forms, *pinch* with thumbs (inside) and fingers (outside) to form the wall. Rotate the bowl and keep pinching all around; the bowl will slowly get bigger. Meet your *pinch pot*.

A pot or figure at this stage is called *greenware*. It is very fragile. You can have it *fired* or baked at more than 500° F in a *kiln*, which is a special oven for pottery. Once fired, the work is called *bisque* ("bisk") or *biscuit*.

Bisque work can be decorated with felt tip pens, acrylic paints, spray paint, shoe polish, wood stains, watercolors, tempera paints, etc. Or you can add a *glaze*, or liquid coating, which is sold in art and craft stores. After dipping in glaze, or having glaze brushed on, the bisque clay is fired again in a kiln. This is called the *glaze firing*.

Clay (and other modelling media) need not be used only for pots and figures. You can make interesting jewelry, wall hangings, and tiles.

You can also buy clay that does not need firing, but dries hard.

Papier-Mâché

This French term means "paper pulp." But not just the French use this technique; so do the Chinese, Japanese, and Mexican people. In America, we borrow papier-mâché ideas from these cultures. The Mexican piñata, a papier-mâché form filled with candy, is especially popular with children.

You can make masks, dolls, life-size statues, globes, etc. You can use the following as armatures (forms) over which to layer the papier-mâché.

A liquid detergent bottle is the right shape for table-top small statues of people. Add dirt to the bottle for stability. Also for table-top-sized objects, build on empty paper milk cartons, plastic butter tubs, styrofoam pieces taped together, paper towel tubes, disposable plastic plates, bowls, and cups.

Round armatures can be inflated baloons, styrofoam balls, and two disposable plastic bowls taped together. If more weight is needed, roll newspapers into a round shape and secure with masking tape.

The Procedure: Cut or tear newspapers into strips about ½" wide. Dip strips into one of the mixtures described on page 81. Place the strips around the armature (form). Put on at least 3 layers of strips, alternating the direction of the strips. If you want a "pretty" top layer, use strips of white paper toweling for that.

Air dry for about 3 days. Paint entire piece with a base coat of white paint. After that dries, decorate with acrylic paints or tempera paints. If tempera is used, finish the piece with spray plastic.

Papier-mâché Mixtures

Wallpaper paste thinned with water

or

Flour paste made from 2 cups water
+ ½ cup flour + 1 T. salt

or

Diluted white glue made from
1 cup glue + 1 cup water

or

Liquid starch (do not dilute)

Handmade Paper

The commercial recipe for paper calls for such things as sawdust and wood shavings, corn husks, weeds, leaves, and bark. The fibers are mashed and then boiled with water to form a mixture called slurry.

To understand the mechanics of making paper, you can mix a slurry with just torn pieces of newspaper — thus, you will recycle paper, not make new paper from scratch.

Soak the pieces of newspaper for several hours in water. From the side of the pan, slip in a square piece of screening (the metal sort that is used in screen windows and doors) so that it goes under the slurry. Slowly lift the screen so that the slurry comes out of the water on top of the screen. Pat the slurry on top, forcing water to drip out.

Turn the slurry onto a towel so that the screen is on top. Pat with a folded washcloth (through the screen). Remove the washcloth and screen and let the slurry dry on the towel. When it is dry, it will lift off as one piece. Paper!

MACHINES AS MEDIA

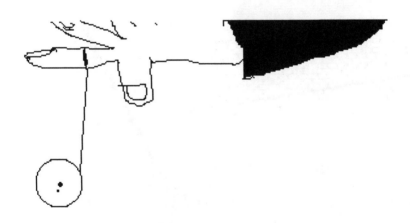

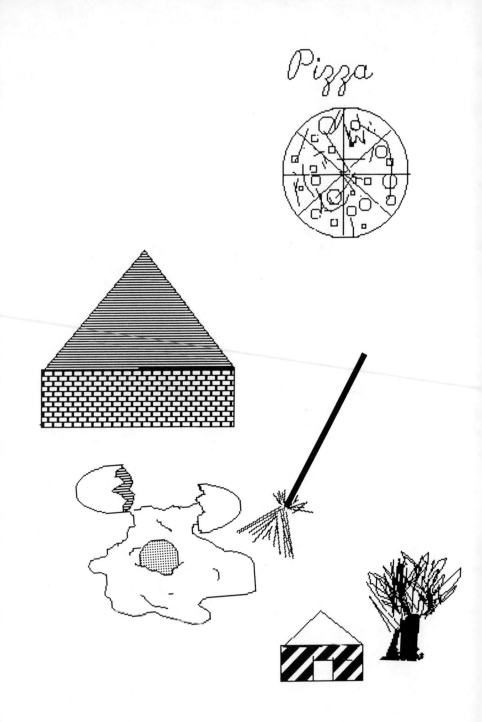

Computer

Since you are growing up with computers at home and at school, you probably have enjoyed computer art already in the form of "paint" programs. If you have printed out greeting cards or stationery, that counts, too. Also, every video game screen is a digitized piece of artwork — that's computer art.

Many adult artists are reluctant to try computer art, but more and more commercial artists are finding it a must. As they become experienced, they grow to like it and appreciate the computer as one more medium.

Computer art is *very* important in desktop publishing. This is the use of computers in producing books, magazines, newsletters, business reports, catalogues, etc. In such publications, the entire design and all artwork can be produced without an artist's hands physically touching the material. Even though the work is done by "remote control" of keyboard, mouse, drawing pad, etc., the talent of the artist is still visible.

The small graphic below is a piece of scanned artwork. That is, it was drawn by hand (pen and ink), then transferred to the computer by a scanner. The scanner "sees" the lines on paper and duplicates them on the computer screen. Once on the screen, the artist can change the drawing many ways ... lighten it, darken it, add a pattern, stretch is wide or tall, flip it over, rotate it, experiment with different colors in it, and on and on.

computer graphics can be words

Cameras

Cameras are so widely used that we tend not to identify them as art media. How lovely! That means that many, many people are using an art medium — when they "shoot" the family vacation, and record the birthday parties, and capture shots of good friends acting goofy.

Of course, most people do not consider themselves photographers or artists, so they don't call their photography art. But if you have admired a "good shot," or smiled over an unusual shadow in a shot, then you've seen art in your photography.

The sort of photography that appears in art museums and galleries is almost always the work of artists who specialize in photography. Some artists limit their work to black and white photography, while some use color, also.

Our most famous American photographer was Ansel Adams. His work is often shown in museums around the country, so watch for it. As often happens in art and other fields, one person can draw enough attention to a type of work to create an enduring interest in that field. Adams did that for photography.

Photography can lead advanced art students into art forms such as film making, print making, and specialized prints such as palladium and platinum prints (which are very expensive).

Pin Hole Camera

Photography using a handmade pin hole camera is very popular with all ages. A pen and ink drawing of such a camera is below.

Some art centers offer courses in pin hole photography. Aside from the cost of the course, the greatest expense in making the camera is the special photography paper used inside it. The actual parts for the camera are recycled materials you can secure at no cost and a single piece of brass available at a hardware store.

You can investigate pin hole cameras on your own, although you may need assistance from an adult occasionally. Your public library can supply the necessary reading material. If you cannot find a book about pin hole photography, ask a librarian to locate one.

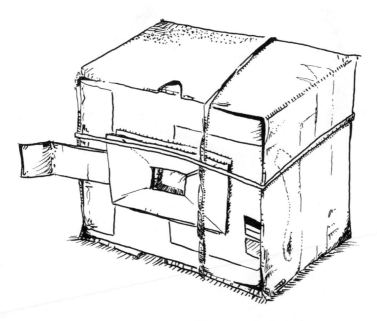

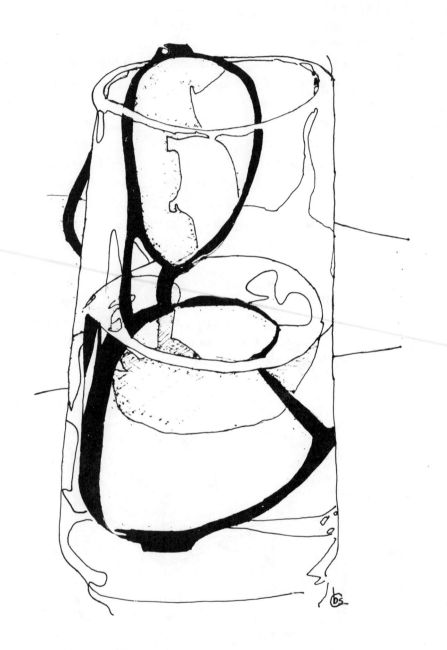

WHAT
ART EDUCATORS
SAY

THIS IS A GESTURE DRAWING BY AN ART STUDENT IN HIGH SCHOOL.

Art Educators

Art educators are sometimes art teachers in schools, but they are also all of these things: college professors, artists teaching classes to adults or children, and artists conducting workshops a few times a year.

Art educators are wonderful resources because they have two ways of looking at things: as artists and as educators. Four art educators shared their thoughts about art for this book.

Barbara Cade is an artist in Hot Springs, Arkansas. She holds her B.A. degree from the University of Illinois and M.A. degree from the University of Washington. She works directly with children as a part-time Artist-in-Residence. Her favorite question for children is, "What do *you* think of it?"

Thad Flenniken is also from Hot Springs, Arkansas. Besides being a well-known artist, he is a professor of art. He holds B.A. and M.F.A. degrees from the University of Arkansas — Fayetteville.

Wayne L. McAfee, B.F.A., M.A., is an Associate Professor of Art at Henderson State University in Arkadelphia, Arkansas. He teaches classes in art for public school art teachers.

Joe T. Scott is also an Associate Professor of Art at Henderson State University. He taught art in public schools for seven years and has taught at the university level for 26 years. He holds B.S.E.: Art, M.Ed. degrees.

What Art Educators Say About...

...viewing artwork in a gallery or museum.

THAD FLENNIKEN

You should stand as close or as far away as you feel necessary. Some things are meant to be viewed closer.

WAYNE MCAFEE

First I look at them far away. After I take it in, then I'll move up real close to look at the brush strokes, the textures, how he did it, this sort of thing. Normally, for just appreciation of a work, you want a certain amount of distance, depending on the size of the work.

BARBARA CADE

Do you have to spend a long time looking at it? Nope.

JOE SCOTT

The same thing is true for sculpture as for paintings: you might want to view it first from all around, at far away distances ... and then get up closer and look at more detail.

What Art Educators Say About...

...touching artwork in museums and galleries.

WAYNE MCAFEE

You should never touch a painting, at all. Your fingers have grease on them and when you touch a painting you deposit some grease that collects dirt ... and paintings cannot be cleaned safely.

Most sculptures, if they're outdoors, you can touch. If they're indoors, it's better not to touch them.

FLASH PHOTOGRAPHY

Flash photography in galleries and museums is not allowed. The light can damage the artwork.

Sometimes, even non-flash photography is outlawed.

Don't be offended if someone asks you to put away your camera. You'll be helping to preserve the artwork.

What Art Educators Say About...

...gallery viewers who say things like "A 2-year-old could have done that," or "I could do that."

Barbara Cade

I was at a show with a friend who said, "I could have done that." I answered, "No, you couldn't have."

What she meant was "I could do that now ... I could copy that."

But I said to her, "You didn't have the original concept. It is very difficult to get all these things meshed together." (It was a kinetic sculpture.)

Then I said, "You didn't do it, either. That's the whole thing: you didn't do it and you couldn't have done it without years of practice!"

Modified Contour Drawing
— not drawn by a 2-year-old

What Art Educators Say About...

...creativity.

JOE SCOTT

We're all born with a certain amount of creativity, or the ability to create. Through adult suppression and criticism we lose a lot of the creativity that, if it were encouraged, would get much stronger. If a young child draws a five-legged cow and paints it purple with green stripes, an adult is going to say "You know that's wrong: a cow has only four legs." And, so, the child — if this happens enough — will say "I can't draw that" just to avoid being criticized.

WAYNE MCAFEE

Creativity really is finding alternatives. The child who paints a rabbit purple? This is an alternative. He paints it purple not because he thinks rabbits are purple but because he likes purple.

THAD FLENNIKEN

Creativity is being able to look at one thing and see something else ... being able to look for and find options that most people don't see, don't know about.

I think everyone is born with creativity. If a person does not grow up in a creative environment, he doesn't necessarily lose it — it becomes dormant. But it can be rekindled or revitalized: a person can rediscover that he is creative.

What Art Educators Say About...

...what is good art.

WAYNE MCAFEE

All art is good art. It comes down to what lasts, what withstands the test of time. Good art is effective. It changes, enhances the lives of people who look at it. I don't like all art. I don't think anybody does. But I recognize the validity of it.

THAD FLENNIKEN

Good art is honest. It is where a person makes an honest, valid effort to personalize a form of expression. If there is communication through that expression, then it is good art.

Good art takes time to develop. It is not an instant thing. People who produce good art develop a sensitivity to the honest approach. It is a skill that requires nurturing and time to evolve.

BARBARA CADE

That word art means too many things. What is good art? The answer depends on your educational level, how much art you've studied, and how much art you've simply looked at. And, finally, your own level of creativity determines your definition of good art.

What Art Educators Say About...

...what is good children's art, and who gets to say.

JOE SCOTT

I think all art done by children is good. As to who gets to say — I don't think it's anybody's business. If the art is strictly a statement from the child, it can't be bad. There may be room for improvement, but who's to say? I don't think it should be judged by adult standards.

WAYNE MCAFEE

When a child does something he's satisfied with, he glows. That's great art.

BARBARA CADE

Unfortunately, who gets to say is usually a parent or adult.

THAD FLENNIKEN

Good art by children is art in which the children choose their own images, express them, make their own choices of color.

What Art Educators Say About...

...young artists around the age of 10 or 11.

JOE SCOTT

At that age they become very critical of their art-work. They want to know how to make things more realistic. Many times, they won't have the ability to do that without further training. They need an awful lot of encouragement from teachers and from parents to work at it and to satisfy themselves.

WAYNE MCAFEE

There's a problem with too many adults and a lot of teachers placing emphasis on the product rather than on the process. One thing the teacher can do, and the parents, too, is to let the child know that what he or she is doing is not wrong. It's perfectly normal for their age. Children this age should not lower their expectations, but should be more realistic about them.

THAD FLENNIKEN

Up to age 10 a child may not have the coordination to do what he would really like to do. After age 10 the coordination is there but most children are not encouraged to seek imagery that is based on very close or astute observation. An interesting thing happens if you expose children this age to the concept of seeing what is actually there: they start to draw things that are very representational. It's like lighting a fire under them. They can't believe they have this capability and it's very exciting for them.

What Art Educators Say About...

...art.

Barbara Cade

*The best thing about art — and the thing that I
liked most about it at the very beginning — was that I
realized that nobody could tell me that it was wrong. I
could make a piece of art and nobody could say it's wrong.*

NOT EVERY DRAWING NEED BE FINISHED.
THIS ONE BECAME AN EXERCISE IN DRAWING EYES.

Contributing Illustrators

Joshua Small

pages 5, 83, 84

Chris Reed

pages 17, 19, 47

Julia Andersen

page 22

Chad Williams

pages 23, 54

Lynda Lyon

page 29 & Back page

Angie Coyle

pages 30, 31

Lori Tyler

pages 45, 59, 94

Chris Meeks

pages 51, 63, 64, 66, 102

Jay Dicus

pages 61, 69, 70, 79, 87

Robbie Harris

pages 62, 90

Tad Roberts

page 63

Chris Harvey

page 77

ABOUT THE AUTHOR

carol brown small's name appears in lower-case letters because that is how she signs it on artwork. In her lifetime, she has signed art as

Muffet Brown   *cbs*   *cbs*
Carol Brown   *Carol Brown Small*
Carol Small   *carol brown small*

Her artwork has changed a lot during her lifetime, also. Of course, age has something to do with some changes, but Carol believes that most changes have come about because she is open to new ideas. She enjoys learning about all forms of art and is willing to experiment.

Her favorite media are paint on plaster, watercolors, and layered oil paint glazes. But she enjoys and works in many other media.

Professionally, Carol has exhibited in art shows, entered juried shows, won juried shows, illustrated books, designed catalogues, illustrated magazine ads, designed ads for billboards, designed logos for businesses, designed a museum exhibit, and taught art.

Her artwork is sold in art museum shops and galleries.

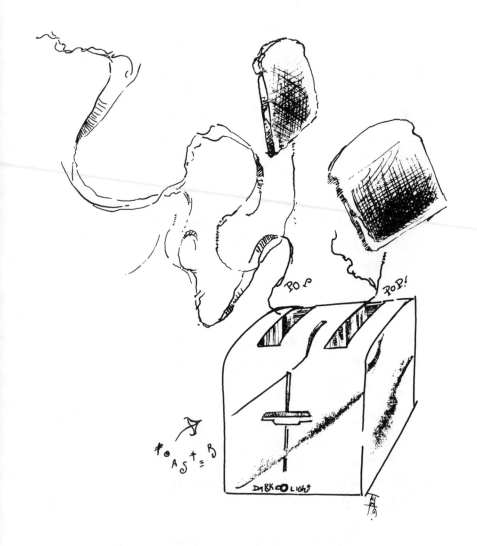

INDEX

103

OTHER BOOKS IN THE CHILDREN'S RESOURCES SERIES

Handmade Christmas Gifts
That Are Actually Usable

ISBN 0-938267-03-5

Publish Your Own Book:
A Resource Book for Young Authors

ISBN 0-938267-02-7

How to Improve Your Mind
Over Summer Vacation

ISBN 0-938267-05-1

Travel-Ogs:
The do it yourself survival kit
for traveling with parents, siblings,
and dirty socks.

ISBN 0-938267-06-X

Bold Productions
P.O. Box 152281
Arlington, Texas 76015
(817) 468-9924

— LYNDA LYON